CHILDHOOD RHYTHMS

A Program of Rhythmic Activities
for
Children of Elementary School Age

by

RUTH EVANS, Sc.D.
*Director of Physical Education
for Women, Springfield College,
Springfield, Massachusetts*

EMMA BATTIS, M.Ed.
*Public Schools,
Springfield, Massachusetts*

CHARTWELL HOUSE, INC.
280 MADISON AVENUE NEW YORK 16, N. Y.

PREFACE

The success of a program of childhood rhythms depends largely on the degree to which it meets the needs, satisfies the interests, and challenges the abilities of children. The real responsibility for all program planning in education rests on the teacher. In order to plan an adequate program of rhythmics for young children, a teacher should have access to many and varied resources. The constant repetition of a limited number of activities in any area is likely to lessen the interest of children in that area. It is true that security is often established through the enjoyment of practicing skills already learned; however, the love of exploration is also strong in young Americans, and the need for something new is ever present.

This book attempts to meet the everyday needs of classroom teachers and teachers of physical education in planning and conducting programs of childhood rhythms. Part I presents a brief statement of philosophy, and also includes suggestions for teachers. Part II, which comprises the main body of the text, takes the form of a substantial collection of widely varied instructional materials suitable for use with children of elementary school age. These materials are the product of many years of experience in the field of elementary education. The activities are simple and practical in nature. They are classified according to an easily understood plan. There is piano music for each activity, as well as reference to a corresponding suitable phonograph recording of *Childhood Rhythms* records.* Where words are essential, as in singing games, they appear with the piano music. In the case of such activities as entail the use of set

Childhood Rhythms records are obtainable from Chartwell House, Inc., 280 Madison Avenue, New York 16, N. Y.

3

4

patterns of movement, directions for these movement patterns are included in the text.

There is no intent to convey the impression that this book presents a complete and final program in childhood rhythms. Rather, the purpose is to present suggestions which may stimulate teachers to create and select many activities never before thought of by them for use with their students.

The authors express their deep gratitude to the many teachers and children, who, over a period of many years, so willingly gave their cooperation in the selection and evaluation of the materials which make up the program suggested in this book. It is hoped that many more teachers and children may find pleasure and profit in the use of these many activities. Gratitude is expressed, also, to Nicholas Tawa, who edited the musical selections and prepared the music manuscript.

RUTH EVANS
EMMA BATTIS

CONTENTS

CONTENTS

SECTION B.   Animal Rhythms

CONTENTS

Childhood Rhythms Records

Childhood Rhythms Records

SECTION F.   Movement in Time and Space

SECTION G.   Ball Bouncing and Rope Jumping

CONTENTS

Part I

RHYTHMIC ACTIVITY IN CHILDHOOD EDUCATION

RHYTHMIC ACTIVITY

The Values of Rhythmic Activity

The contribution made by rhythmic activity to child growth and development cannot be overestimated. Current educational philosophy recognizes this contribution and makes rhythmic activity a major area of learning for children in nursery school, kindergarten, and elementary school. Especially during their first few years in school, children today spend considerable time participating in activities based on response to music and rhythm. It is quite generally accepted that all children have natural ability, at least to some degree, to make this response. Most teachers of young children agree that there is no truth in the statement that some children have "no sense of rhythm." What is lacking, sometimes, is the desire or the capacity to translate into movement this feeling for response to rhythm. The activities which provide children with opportunity to strengthen their rhythmic response are essentially physical in nature; nevertheless, in some school situations rhythmics are a part of the physical education program, while in other instances they are designated as music education. Actually it makes little difference where this area of learning is placed in the total curriculum. The important thing is that it be given equal consideration with other essential subject matter fields.

Placing emphasis on rhythmic activity is one way in which education may provide realistic and pleasurable experiences for children. The learning which takes place in a well-planned program of rhythmic activities is not limited to the development of motor skills and neuromuscular coordinations, important though this is. As a matter of fact, perfection of movement is by no means a primary objective of the program. Natural, free movement is the first desired result. Rhythmic activity provides children with many experiences favorable to social development and adjustment. Learning to listen is as important as learning to respond to music. Naturally, young children demonstrate greater interest in body movement and physical activity than they do in listening. But in order for them to learn to recognize and interpret musical meter and mood, listening must precede response. It is not necessary for young children to learn the technical aspects of music. But, if they are to achieve skill at responding to musical tempo and spirit, they must first feel the mood of the musical composition which is being used. The enthusiasm of children for vigorous physical activity and their need for being active may be easily satisfied by participation in the rhythmic activity program. And this program provides recreation, too. The repetition of movement patterns which children have developed through response to music is fun. And fun is essential to a good program of education for children.

Individual Response to Rhythm

Learning to respond to musical rhythm helps to establish in children self-confidence and poise, two qualities essential to personality development. The child who, at an early age, experiences the vigorous participation which is typical of the program of rhythmic activity learns to move and to use his body efficiently. He escapes, at least to a considerable degree, the self-consciousness so often suffered by those who do not know the joy of moving in response to music; marching to a martial air, swaying or swinging to music which suggests such movement, running or skipping to the lilt of lively tunes. Through such participation in rhythmic activities children develop respect for their own ideas. If the climate for learning is favorable, each child comes to realize that his own interpretation of or reaction to musical meter is just as important as the interpretations and reactions of others. This helps to build self-respect.

Group Response to Rhythm

Moving alone helps to develop self-confidence, while moving with others in response to musical rhythm serves to develop in children a sense of belonging and security. Joining hands in a circle may be the very thing that dispels loneliness among children just entering kindergarten. Running or skipping with a partner may help to build in many children the belief that they are "wanted." Coordinating the ideas and reactions of one individual with the ideas and reactions of others in the group facilitates good social adjustment. And children learn quite easily through observing and imitating others; often they take great pleasure in this type of learning.

Group consciousness does not just happen; it must be carefully planned in order that the desired results accrue. Group activity in rhythmics provides many experiences in which youngsters may learn to share privileges and responsibilities with others, and also to share ideas for interpretation. Very early in this program of rhythmic activity children realize the need for consideration of others even in such a simple matter as the use of space. They learn to move *with* rather than *against* the group. Some young persons who find it difficult to cooperate with others learn for the first time to enjoy group association while playing a singing game or while waddling like ducks in response to music.

The Scope and Sequence of Childhood Rhythms

Childhood education concerns itself with the needs and interests which, if met and fulfilled, contribute to the growth and development of children. Each child grows according to an individual or personal pattern in ways that are physical, mental, social, and emotional. Some children grow and develop faster in one direction, some in another. There are, it is true, certain basic factors which are similar in the growth and development of all children. But the fact remains that there can be no clear-cut line of demarcation between the age characteristics or growth stages of children from one year to another. There is no real authority for claiming that all five-year-old children should be just so many inches tall, or that these children should attain identical standards of reading ability, or likewise the same standard of accuracy in response to musical rhythm. It seems desirable, in planning a program of rhythmic activity for elementary-school-age children, to group the materials of instruction according to a simple classification which allows for (1) activities for children from five to eight years, and (2) activities for children from nine to twelve years.

Children in the five- to eight-year-old group are possessed of a strong drive or urge for physical activity. They want to be "on the go" all the time. For purposes of physical growth they need this physical activity, but because they tire rather quickly, and because their interest span is short, the periods of activity for this group should be of fairly short duration, should be scheduled frequently, and should be balanced with periods of rest and relaxation. Children of this age group are friendly, yet individualistic and possessive. They need many group experiences in order to develop desirable social traits. Imagination and the love of "make believe" are strong in children from five to eight years of age. Role playing is very important to them. All this means that the program of rhythmic activity for the younger children in elementary schools should be planned to include (1) vigorous physical activity balanced with rest, (2) group activities as well as individual activities, and (3) dramatic and interpretative activities.

Children in the nine- to twelve-year-old range resemble the younger elementary school group in that they continue to develop as individuals, yet in certain ways these individuals are quite similar to each other. During these years in the upper elementary school grades physical growth may be rapid; this accounts, no doubt, for the fact that some of these children are awkward and self-conscious. Individual differences of all sorts are apparent here, but these children show strong desires to "belong." They want to be a part of the group in which they find themselves. They want the approval of their peers. There is also a persistent desire on the part of children in this age range to perfect skills. There is probably no less imagination at this age level, but there is greater sense of realism than is found in younger children. These older children want to know the reasons for, the background of, the rules involved in the activities in which they participate. There is present at this age a preference among boys to associate with boys, and for girls to associate with girls. But there is need for participation in activities involving both boys and girls. In summary, then, the factors essential to the planning of a rhythmic activities program for the nine to twelve-year-old group are (1) the need for providing experiences involving the practice of skills that will eliminate awkwardness and self-consciousness, (2) group activities which include opportunities for boys and girls to participate together, and (3) activities involving definite and challenging skills.

Teaching Suggestions

There is no one best method to be applied to the teaching of rhythmic activities. In fact, there is no one best way of teaching anything. The method which brings about the desired results is the one to use in any situation. In this field of childhood rhythms, however, certain procedures seem to facilitate favorable and satisfactory results. A number of these procedures are suggested here.

Much has been said and written concerning the use of the creative approach in the teaching of rhythmic activities. But the term "creative" has often been interpreted incorrectly. Actually, any activity which is new to the learner represents creative experience. The learner's own interpretation makes his performance of a skill an individual and creative matter. In the field of rhythmics a lack of understanding of this point may limit the meaning of the word "creative" to purely and immediately original activities. This narrow interpretation has, to a degree at least, caused confusion which has sometimes resulted in the use of methods which prove to be quite unsatisfactory and unsuitable. "Do what the music tells you," an expression used sometimes to encourage children to respond with interpretative movement to musical rhythm may at times convey little or no meaning to the group. Actually, until they become experienced in reacting to musical mood and meter, children often find themselves without much to "do to the music." What happens in many such situations is that one child may have an idea for interpretation, and all others may follow his lead.

Children sometimes need, and often enjoy, direction and guidance. The questions, "What shall I do?" and "How shall I do it?" prove this point. Children usually react favorably to direction if the direction is not domination. Teachers should direct children when the need for such direction is indicated, but they should also encourage children to direct themselves. To introduce a simple rhythmic activity by saying, "This is walking music. Let's walk to it," is suitable procedure, provided that this leadership serves as a springboard to self-direction. For example, when a fundamental rhythm such as walking is being taught, the following steps in progression are suggested: (1) directing children to respond to the rhythm of the musical selection by walking in time to the metric beat, but each child in his own way, (2) providing other selections which suggest the same response, and (3) teaching children to recognize as walking music other selections which might be suitable. The use of these steps in teaching provides opportunity for teacher leadership which leads to self-direction.

After children become accustomed, through various experiences, to reacting and responding to musical rhythm the need for teacher leadership decreases, and the opportunities for self-direction become more numerous. Day by day, as experiences broaden, children suggest more and more ideas for interpretation. Teachers should make full use of these suggestions and arrange sufficient opportunity for the development of ideas. Seasonal suggestions throughout the year furnish inspiration and background for excellent program planning. Toys at Christmas, winter sports during their season, animals at any season, circuses in the spring, are all examples of such suggestions. Class excursions, a visit to a railroad station, and a bus ride provide subject matter for a lesson in rhythmic activity. Seeing an airplane fly over the school may inspire children to want to dramatize the swift movement across the sky.

A few fundamental principles are listed here which may prove to be of value to teachers of children in elementary schools in planning and presenting programs of rhythmic activity:

(1) There should be opportunity for all children in the group to participate in vigorous physical activity, followed by rest.

(2) Each child in the group should have opportunity to suggest interpretation and movement.

(3) Movement patterns suggested by children should develop into activities which may be carried on by the group.

(4) Each lesson should make a contribution to social living by providing group experience.

(5) There should be sufficient variety of activity in each lesson to hold the interest of the group. Care should be taken, however, not to sacrifice real learning for the sake of variety.

(6) Each lesson should be a pleasant experience for the children.

(7) Each lesson should be evaluated by the teacher and the class.

(8) The rhythmic activity lesson should be long enough to make possible real achievement, but not so long that children become overfatigued. The period should be twenty minutes to a half-hour.

(9) The music used should be simple and the rhythm sufficiently marked so that children will easily feel the swing and the mood of the selection to which they are expected to react.

98477

Part II

SUGGESTED TEACHING MATERIALS

FUNDAMENTAL RHYTHMS

Galloping

Childhood Rhythms Records*
Series I, Record 101-102

* *Childhood Rhythms* records are obtainable from Chartwell House, Inc., 280 Madison Avenue, New York 16, N. Y.

Childhood Rhythms Records
Series I, Record 101-102

ALLEGRETTO (♩ = 92)

CHILDHOOD RHYTHMS

Marching

Childhood Rhythms Records
Series I, Record 101-102

ALLEGRO VIVACE (♩.=136)

Running I

Childhood Rhythms Records
Series I, Record 101-102

Running II

Childhood Rhythms Records
Series III, Record 303-304

ALLEGRO (♩ = 104)

Skipping I

Childhood Rhythms Records
Series I, Record 101-102

ALLEGRO ($\quad$ = 104)

Skipping II

Childhood Rhythms Records
Series I, Record 101-102

ALLEGRO (♩.=104)

Skipping III

Childhood Rhythms Records
Series III, Record 303-304

NON TROPPO ALLEGRO ($\bullet$ = 96)

Sliding

Childhood Rhythms Records
Series V, Record 505-506

ALLEGRETTO ($\flat$ = 88)

Walking I

Childhood Rhythms Records
Series I, Record 101-102

NON TROPPO (♩ = 108)

Walking II

Childhood Rhythms Records
Series III, Record 303-304

NON TROPPO (♩=108)

Section B

ANIMAL RHYTHMS

Bears

Childhood Rhythms Records
Series V, Record 501-502

MODERATO (♩. = 76)

Birds

Childhood Rhythms Records
Series IX, Record 901-902

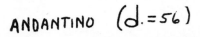

Camels

Childhood Rhythms Records
Series I, Record 103-104

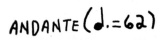

Chickens

Childhood Rhythms Records
Series V, Record 501-502

POCO PRESTO (♩=138)

Ducks

Childhood Rhythms Records
Series I, Record 103-104

CHILDHOOD RHYTHMS

Elephants

Childhood Rhythms Records
Series I, Record 103-104

RISOLUTO (♩.=66)

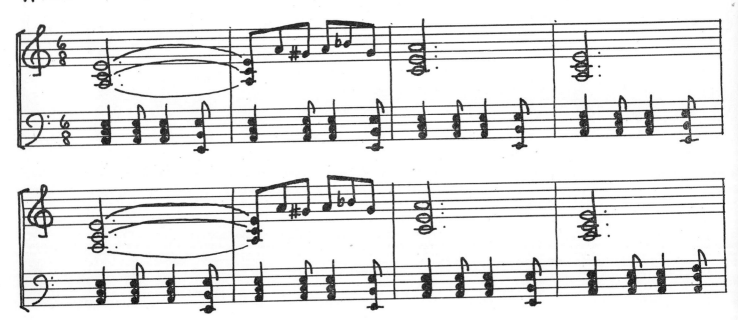

Frogs

Childhood Rhythms Records
Series V, Record 501-502

Giraffes

Childhood Rhythms Records
Series IX, Record 901-902

ALLEGRO MODERATO (♩=100)

CHILDHOOD RHYTHMS

Horses (High Stepping)

Childhood Rhythms Records
Series I, Record 103-104

Horses (Trotting)

Childhood Rhythms Records
Series IX, Record 901-902

PRESTO (♩=152)

CHILDHOOD RHYTHMS

Kangaroos

Childhood Rhythms Records
Series IX, Record 901-902

ALLEGRO (♩=104)

Monkeys

Childhood Rhythms Records
Series IX, Record 901-902

Penguins

Childhood Rhythms Records
Series IX, Record 901-902

ALLEGRO (♩=120)

Rabbits

Childhood Rhythms Records
Series V, Record 501-502

VIVACE (♩=132)

Section C

PLAY RHYTHMS AND STUNTS

Airplanes

Childhood Rhythms Records
Series I, Record 103-104

67

Bicycles

Childhood Rhythms Records
Series I, Record 105-106

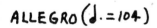

CHILDHOOD RHYTHMS

Cartwheels

Childhood Rhythms Records
Series V, Record 503-504

MODERATO (♩.=58)

Church Bells

Childhood Rhythms Records
Series IX, Record 903-904

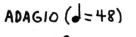

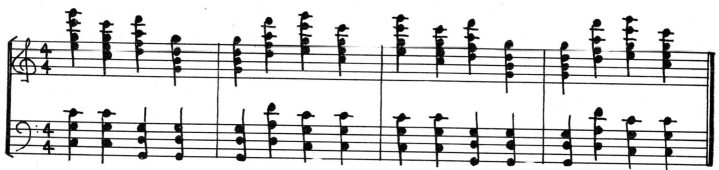

CHILDHOOD RHYTHMS

Climbing (Stairs or Ladder)

Childhood Rhythms Records
Series IX, Record 905-906

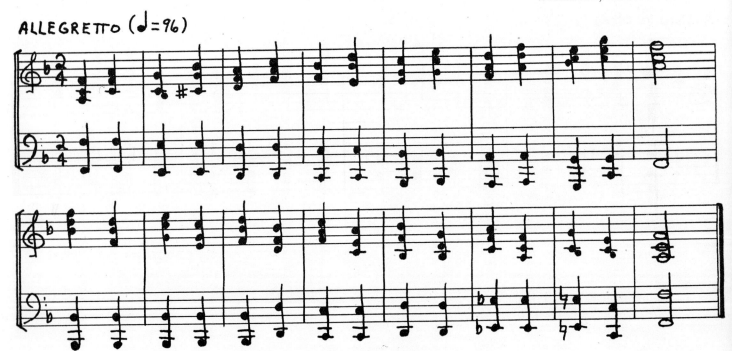

Clocks

Childhood Rhythms Records
Series II, Record 205-206

Elevators

Childhood Rhythms Records
Series II, Record 205-206

Jumping Jacks

Childhood Rhythms Records
Series II, Record 205-206

MODERATO (♩.=84)

CHILDHOOD RHYTHMS

Rowboats

Childhood Rhythms Records
Series I, Record 105-106

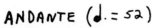

See Saws

Childhood Rhythms Records
Series I, Record 105-106

MODERATO (♩.=63)

CHILDHOOD RHYTHMS

Sit Up and Lie Down

Childhood Rhythms Records
Series V, Record 503-504

ANDANTINO ($\quad$ = 88)

Skating

Childhood Rhythms Records
Series V, Record 505-506

MODERATO (♩.=63)

Somersaults

Childhood Rhythms Records
Series V, Record 503-504

Sleigh Bells

Childhood Rhythms Records
Series IX, Record 903-904

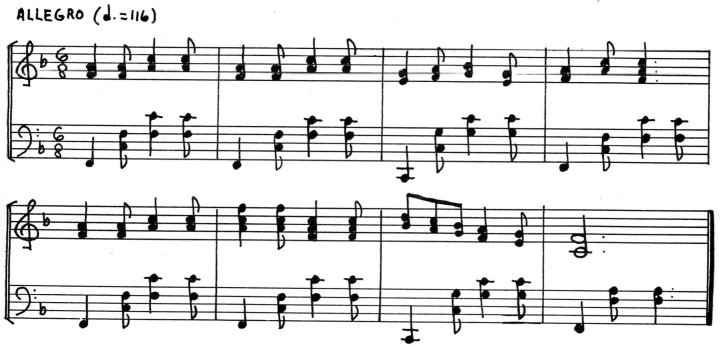

CHILDHOOD RHYTHMS

Swings

Childhood Rhythms Records
Series I, Record 105-106

MODERATO (♩.=60)

Tin Soldiers

Childhood Rhythms Records
Series I, Record 103-104

Tops

Childhood Rhythms Records
Series I, Record 103-104

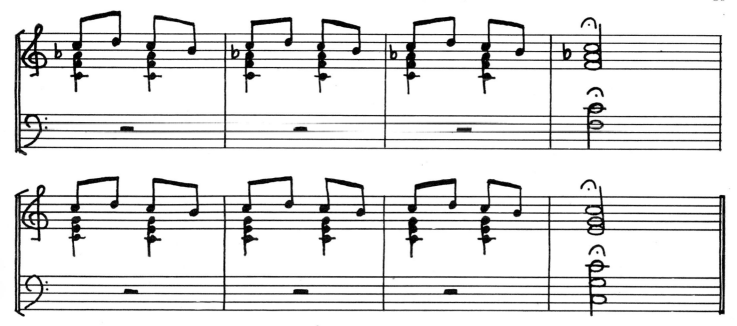

Trains

Childhood Rhythms Records
Series I, Record 103-104

ADAGIO - PRESTO - ADAGIO

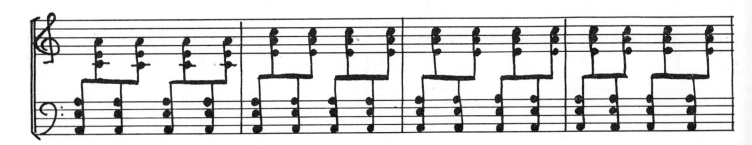

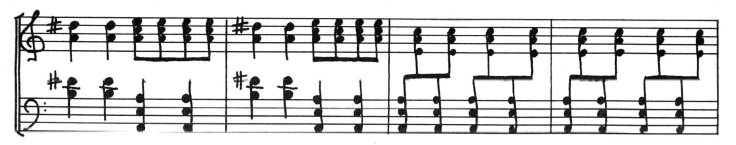

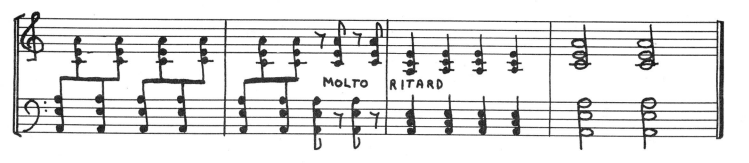

CHARACTER RHYTHMS

Clowns

Childhood Rhythms Records
Series IX, Record 903-904

ALLEGRETTO ($\,\cdot$=84)

Cowboys

Childhood Rhythms Records
Series V, Record 501-502

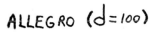

Dolls

Childhood Rhythms Records
Series IX, Record 903-904

ALLEGRO (♩= 96)

Dwarfs

Childhood Rhythms Records
Series I, Record 105-106

Fairies

Childhood Rhythms Records
Series I, Record 105-106

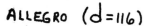

Giants

Childhood Rhythms Records
Series I, Record 105-106

CHILDHOOD RHYTHMS

Goblins

Childhood Rhythms Records
Series IX, Record 903-904

ALLEGRO MODERATO (♩=108)

Indians

Childhood Rhythms Records
Series V, Record 501-502

PRESTO (♩=176)

Sailors

Childhood Rhythms Records
Series V, Record 501-502

ALLEGRO (♩=116)

CHILDHOOD RHYTHMS

Soldiers

Childhood Rhythms Records
Series V, Record 501-502

ALLEGRO (♩.=116)

Witches

Childhood Rhythms Records
Series I, Record 105-106

ALLEGRO NON TROPPO (♩ = 96)

DANCE STEPS AND RHYTHMS

Balance

Childhood Rhythms Records
Series IX, Record 905-906

MODERATO (♩. = 56)

MEASURES

1   Easy, smooth movement forward, backward or sideward (count 1).

Step forward (or sideward) with one foot, bring the other foot to the one just stepped with (count 2), rise on toes and come down on heels (count 3).

Jig

Childhood Rhythms Records
Series IX, Record 905-906

ALLEGRO (♩.=104)

Any hopping, jumping, lively step that fits the beat of the music. Children may wish to dance this alone or with partners.

Heel and Toe

Childhood Rhythms Records
Series II, Record 205-206

MEASURES

1   Point the right foot forward, heel down (count 1), then place the same foot behind the left foot, toe down (count 2).

1   Run three steps (right, left, right).

Repeat as many times as the music allows.

Mazurka

Childhood Rhythms Records
Series III, Record 303-304

MEASURES

    1   Slide diagonally forward with the right foot (count 1), bring the left foot to the right (count 2), hop on the left foot, raising the right foot forward (count 3).

    1   Continue with the same foot. When a change to the other foot is desired make this change by using the last measure of a musical phrase for three stamping steps.

Polka

Childhood Rhythms Records
Series III, Record 303-304

ALLEGRO MODERATO ($\quad$=100)

MEASURES

1   Hop on the left foot, raising the right (count and), step forward or to the side with the right foot (count 1), bring the left foot to the right (count and), step again with the right foot (count 2).

Continue alternately left and right.

Prancing

Childhood Rhythms Records
Series V, Record 505-506

Schottische

Childhood Rhythms Records
Series III, Record 303-304

ALLEGRO NON TROPPO (♩=96)

Measures

1   Step forward or to the side with the right foot (count 1), bring the left foot to the right (count 2), step again with the right foot (count 3), hop on the right foot, raising the left (count 4).

        Continue alternately left and right.

CHILDHOOD RHYTHMS

Step and Point

Childhood Rhythms Records
Series II, Record 205-206

ALLEGRETTO (♩ =88)

Tip Toe

Childhood Rhythms Records
Series IX, Record 905-906

CHILDHOOD RHYTHMS

Two Step

Childhood Rhythms Records
Series IX, Record 903-904

MEASURES

    1   Step forward or to the side with the right foot (count 1), bring the left foot to the right (count and), step again with the right foot (count 2).

    Continue alternately left and right.

Section F

MOVEMENT IN TIME AND SPACE

Accented Run

Childhood Rhythms Records
Series IX, Record 905-906

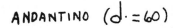

125

Fast and Slow

Childhood Rhythms Records
Series II, Record 201-202

MOVEMENT IN TIME AND SPACE

Pendulum Swing

Childhood Rhythms Records
Series IX, Record 905-906

ANDANTINO ($\bullet\cdot$ =60)

Round and Round

Childhood Rhythms Records
Series II, Record 201-202

ALLEGRETTO (♩.=84)

Run and Hop

Childhood Rhythms Records
Series II, Record 201-202

MOLTO ALLEGRO (♩=152)

CHILDHOOD RHYTHMS

Stretch and Fold

Childhood Rhythms Records
Series V, Record 505-506

ANDANTINO (♩ = 72)

Sway and Twist

Childhood Rhythms Records
Series V, Record 505-506

ANDANTE (♩. = 54)

Under Your Arms

Childhood Rhythms Records
Series V, Record 505-506

FORMATION

Partners facing with both hands joined.

MEASURES

1   Swing both arms to one side and return.

1   Swing again to the same side and turn away from partners, moving under both arms.
      Do not release hands at any time during the swings.

Up and Down

Childhood Rhythms Records
Series II, Record 201-202

Walk and Bow (*Minuet*)

Childhood Rhythms Records
Series II, Record 205-206

ALLEGRETTO (♩=88)

FORMATION

Double circle, partners side by side, inside hands joined (boys on left of girls).

Any combination of walking steps and bows that fits the music. This rhythm provides a foundation for simple minuet patterns.

MEASURES

2   Starting with the inside foot, walk forward three steps, then face partners and bow.

2   Repeat, starting with the outside foot.

2   Face partners, join right hands. Walk three steps around partner, then stop and bow.

2   Repeat the last two measures.
      Repeat all as many times as the music will permit.

Walk and Hop

Childhood Rhythms Records
Series II, Record 201-202

Walk and Skip

Childhood Rhythms Records
Series II, Record 201-202

Section G

BALL BOUNCING AND ROPE JUMPING

Ball Rolling

Childhood Rhythms Records
Series V, Record 503-504

140

Bounce and Hold

Childhood Rhythms Records
Series II, Record 203-204

ALLEGRETTO (♩=88)

CHILDHOOD RHYTHMS

Bounce, Bounce, Bounce, and Hold

Childhood Rhythms Records
Series II, Record 203-204

Combination Bounce

Childhood Rhythms Records
Series II, Record 203-204

One, Two, Three Alairy

Childhood Rhythms Records
Series V, Record 503-504

ALLEGRO MODERATO (♩=96)

CHILDHOOD RHYTHMS

Slow Bounce

Childhood Rhythms Records
Series V, Record 503-504

Fast Jump (*Pepper*)

Childhood Rhythms Records
Series II, Record 203-204

Jump in Place

Childhood Rhythms Records
Series II, Record 203-204

ALLEGRO (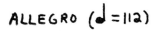=112)

Rope Skipping

Childhood Rhythms Records
Series II, Record 203-204

ALLEGRO (♩. =100)

SINGING GAMES

Ach! Ja

Childhood Rhythms Records
Series VII, Record 705-706

MOLTO ALLEGRO (♩=138)

154

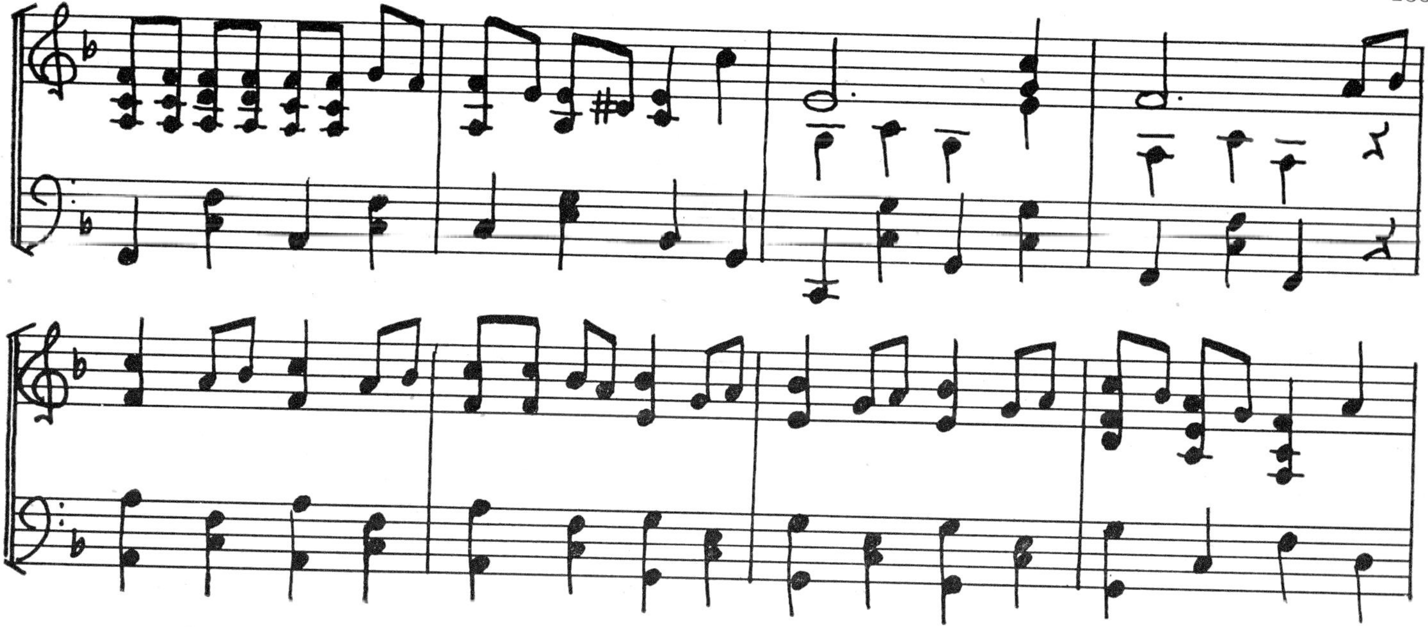

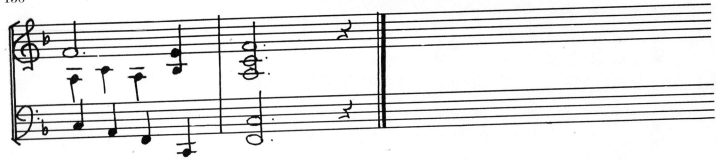

FORMATION

Double circle, partners side by side facing counterclockwise, with inside hands joined.

Sing as you dance

MEASURES

2   "The mother and the father take the children to the fair"
All walk forward in time to the music, starting with the outside foot (eight steps).

2   "Ach, Ja! Ach, Ja!"
Partners drop hands and bow to each other twice.

2   "They haven't any money but they're rich as any there"
All face clockwise and walk forward (eight steps).

2   "Ach, Ja! Ach, Ja!"
Partners drop hands and bow to each other twice.

2   "Tra la la, tra la la, tra la la la la la la"
Partners face each other, join both hands and take two slow slides then three faster slides counterclockwise.

2   "Tra la la, Tra la la, Tra la la la la la la la"
Repeat last two measures, moving clockwise.

2   "Ach, Ja! Ach, Ja."
Partners drop hands and bow to each other twice.

Before starting again each boy move forward to the next girl.

CHILDHOOD RHYTHMS

Bow, Bow, Belinda

Childhood Rhythms Records
Series VII, Record 705-706

ALLEGRO VIVACE (♩=144)

FORMATION

Double circle, partners facing.

Sing as you dance

MEASURES

"Step and step and bow, Belinda
Step and step and bow, Belinda
Step and step and bow, Belinda
Won't you be my partner?"

2   All take three steps forward toward partner and bow.

2   Take three steps back to place and bow.

2   Take three steps forward again and bow.

2   Take three steps back to place and bow.

8   "Right hands round and swing Belinda"
Repeat this line three times, then finish verse with the line, "Won't you be my partner?" Follow the action suggested by the words.

8   "Left hands round and swing Belinda"
Repeat this line three times, then finish verse with the line, "Won't you be my partner?" Follow the action suggested by the words.

8   "Both hands round and swing Belinda"
Repeat as above, only swinging both hands.

8   "Right hands round and swing Belinda
Left hands round and swing Belinda
Both hands round and swing Belinda
Promenade, Belinda."

Follow the actions suggested by the words, as in previous verses, then partners join hands, face counterclockwise, and walk forward four steps.

Push the Business On

Childhood Rhythms Records
Series VI, Record 601-602

ALLEGRO (♩. =108)

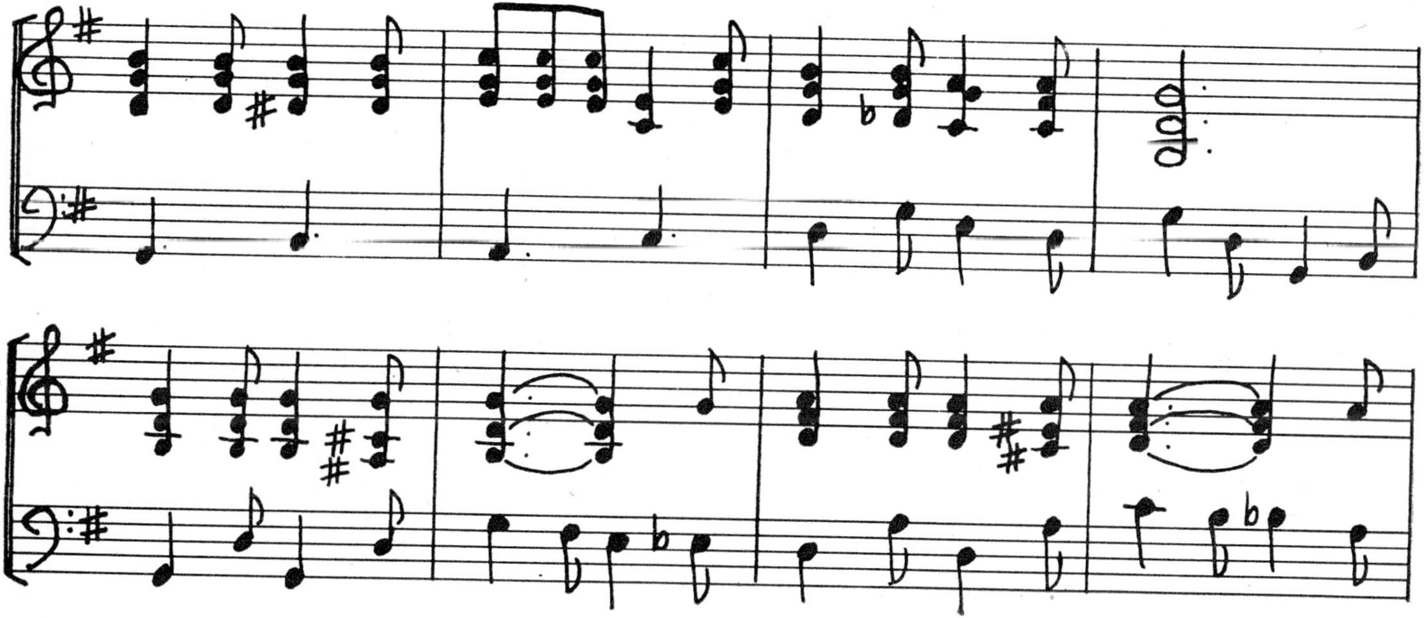

FORMATION

Double circle, partners side by side with inside hands joined, facing counterclockwise.

Sing as you dance

MEASURES

8   "We'll hire a horse and hire a gig
         So all the world may dance a jig
         And I'll do all that ever I can
         To push the business on"
      Walk around the circle.

4   "To push the business on
         To push the business on"
      Clap hands three times, stop, and clap three times again.

4   "And I'll do all that ever I can
           To push the business on"
      Partners join both hands, walk four steps around each other to place, then girls continue walking
four more steps to join the next boy.

      Repeat all with new partner.

Saturday Afternoon

Childhood Rhythms Records
Series VI, Record 605-606

FORMATION

Single circle, all facing center. One child stands in the center of the circle to start the game.

Sing as you play

MEASURES

8   "Mary went to Sally's house, Sally's house, Sally's house
          Mary went to Sally's house, on Saturday afternoon"
The child in the center of the circle whose name might be Mary (if it is not, then the child's own name should be sung) skips around inside the circle while the group sings the words in the verse.

8   "Sally, won't you play with me, play with me, play with me?
          Sally, won't you play with me on Saturday afternoon?"
All clap in time to the music. The child who has been skipping stops in front of Sally (or any other

child), makes a bow, joins hands with this child, then the two children skip around inside the circle. The first child then returns to a place in the circle, while the second child starts the game again.

This is valuable as a "get acquainted" game.

Skip Around Your Partner

Childhood Rhythms Records
Series VI, Record 603-604

ALLEGRO (♩=116)

FORMATION

    Partners facing

Sing as you dance

MEASURES

2	"Put your hands on your shoulders, put your hands on your knees
2	Your hands on your shoulders, your hands on your knees
2	Put your hands on your shoulders, put your hands on your knees
2	Then skip around your partner"
2	"Reach up to the ceiling and down to the floor,
2	Up to the ceiling and down to the floor
2	Reach up to the ceiling and down to the floor
2	Then skip around your partner"
2	"Bend over this way, bend over that way
2	Bend over this way, bend over that way
2	Bend over this way, bend over that way
2	Then skip around your partner"

Interpret the words with appropriate action and introduce other new words.

Walking with My Partner

Childhood Rhythms Records
Series VI, Record 605-606

FORMATION

Double circle, partners side by side, inside hands joined, all facing counterclockwise.

Sing as you play

MEASURES

8   "Walking, walking, walking with a partner
Walking, walking, walking in a ring."
All walk around the circle with partners.
Repeat, hopping, skipping, running, or with any activity the children select. Substitute in the song the word that describes the action.

NURSERY RHYMES

Crooked Man

Childhood Rhythms Records
Series VII, Record 703-704

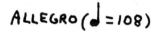

FORMATION

    Single circle, all facing counterclockwise.

Sing as you dance

MEASURES

4   "There was a crooked man who walked a crooked mile
           He found a crooked sixpence upon a crooked stile"
    All walk around the circle, imitating a crooked man.

4   "He found a crooked cat who caught a crooked mouse
           And they all lived together in a little crooked house"
    Repeat the walking in the opposite direction.

Hey, Diddle Diddle

Childhood Rhythms Records
Series VII, Record 703-704

MODERATO (♩.=80)

FORMATION

Double circle with partners side by side facing counterclockwise.

Sing as you dance

MEASURES

2   "Hey, Diddle Diddle, the cat and the fiddle"
All pretend to play fiddles.

2   "The cow jumped over the moon"
All run a few steps around the circle, then jump high in the air.

2   "The little dog laughed to see the fun"
Partners face each other, point to each other and laugh.

2   "And the dish ran away with the spoon"
Partners join inside hands and run around the circle.

Hickory Dickory Dock

Childhood Rhythms Records
Series VII, Record 701-702

ANDANTINO (♩. =66)

FORMATION

All stand in a single circle facing the center, with arms stretched high overhead.

Sing as you dance

MEASURES

2   "Hickory, Dickory, Dock"
All bend to the right, left, right, at the same time stamping right, left, right.

2   "The mouse ran up the clock"
All skip toward the center of the circle.

1   "The clock struck one"
All clap hands over heads.

1   "And down he'd run"
All run back to places.

2   "Hickory, Dickory, Dock"
Stretch arms over heads and bend to the right, left, right, at the same time stamping right, left, right.

8   Children hum the chorus. All join hands and skip eight steps around the circle to the right, then to the left.

Humpty Dumpty

Childhood Rhythms Records
Series VII, Record 701-702

FORMATION

One child (Humpty Dumpty) stands in the center of the room. A group of children (the king's horses) stand on the left side of the room. Another group (the king's men) stand on the right.

Sing as you dance

MEASURES

2   "Humpty Dumpty sat on a wall"
He sits cross-legged on the floor and sways.

2   "Humpty Dumpty had a great fall"
He topples over.

4   "All the king's horses and all the king's men couldn't put Humpty together again"
Horses and men gallop over and try to pick Humpty Dumpty up, but they cannot, so they gallop back to their places.

Little Miss Muffet

Childhood Rhythms Records
Series VII, Record 703-704

ANDANTE (♩. = 63)

FORMATION

Double circle, partners facing.

Sing as you dance

MEASURES

4   "Little Miss Muffet sat on a tuffet
          Eating her curds and whey"
      The girls sit on their heels and pretend to eat, while the boys stoop and pretend to hide.

2   "Along came a spider and sat down beside her"
      Boys creep up softly and stoop, sitting beside the girls.

2   "And frightened Miss Muffet away"
      Girls run to the center of the circle.

Pease Porridge Hot

Childhood Rhythms Records
Series VI, Record 605-606

FORMATION

Double circle, partners facing.

Sing as you dance

MEASURES

2   "Pease porridge hot, pease porridge cold"
Slap sides, clap hands together, then clap partner's hands.

2   "Pease porridge in the pot nine days old"
Slap sides, clap hands together, slap partner's right hand, clap own hands, clap partner's left hand, clap own hands, clap partner's two hands.

2   "Some like it hot, some like it cold"
Repeat first two measures.

2   "Some like it in the pot nine days old"
Repeat second two measures.

8   For the chorus, join both hands with partner, slide around the circle counterclockwise, then clockwise.

Pussy Cat

Childhood Rhythms Records
Series VII, Record 703-704

FORMATION

Any informal grouping.

Sing as you dance

MEASURES

2   "Pussy Cat, Pussy Cat, where have you been?"
           All nod to the left, then to the right, then run forward.

2   "I've been to London to visit the Queen"
           All turn and walk proudly back to place.

2   "Pussy Cat, Pussy Cat, what did you there?"
           All nod to the left, then to the right, then run forward.

2   "I frightened a little mouse under the chair"
           All run forward quickly, skipping on the last step.

Ride a Cock-Horse

Childhood Rhythms Records
Series VII, Record 701-702

FORMATION

    Single circle all facing counterclockwise.

Sing as you dance

    MEASURES

      4   "Ride a cock horse to Banbury Cross
              To see a grand lady upon a white horse"
      All gallop around the circle.

      2   "With rings on her fingers and bells on her toes"
      Lift the left foot and shake it, then lift the right foot and shake it.

      2   "She shall have music wherever she goes"
      All whirl around to the right in place.

Two Little Blackbirds

Childhood Rhythms Records
Series VII, Record 703-704

FORMATION

Double circle, partners facing.

Sing as you dance

MEASURES

4   "Two little blackbirds sitting on a hill"
On the word "sit," all stoop down.

"One named Jack, the other named Jill"
2   On the word "Jack," the boys jump up and stoop down again.
2   On the word "Jill," the girls jump up and stoop down again.

"Fly away, Jack, fly away, Jill"
2   On the word "Jack," the boys fly away from their partners.
2   On the word "Jill," the girls fly away from their partners.

"Come back, Jack, come back, Jill"
2   On the word "Jack," the boys return to their places.
2   On the word "Jill," the girls return to their places.

16   For the chorus, all join hands with partners and skip counterclockwise around the circle.

DANCES FOR CHILDREN

American Country Dance (Turkey in the Straw)

Childhood Rhythms Records
Series IV, Record 401-402

187

FORMATION

Four couples in a set, standing one beside the other, partners facing. (Boys are in a line on one side, girls in a line on the other.)

MEASURES

8   First couple join both hands, take four slides down the center of the set, then four slides up the center of the set to place.

8   All dancers join both hands with partners and skip eight steps around each other to place.

4   Boys all join hands, girls do the same. Starting with the right foot all walk forward four steps then four steps backward to place.

4   Walk forward four steps again. Now partners join both hands high. The first couple takes four slides down the center of the set under the arches made by the joined hands of the other three couples.

Repeat the whole dance three more times, until each couple has been the head couple.

The Broom Dance (German)

Childhood Rhythms Records
Series X, Record 1001-1002

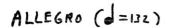

Formation

Double circle, partners side by side, inside hands joined, all facing counterclockwise. One child stands in the center of the circle holding a small broom.

> "One, two, three, four, five, six, seven
> Where's my partner, nine, ten, eleven?
> In Berlin, in Stettin
> That's the place to find him in"

Measures

8   All march around the circle. The child in the center hands the broom to another child and joins hands with this child's partner. The child who now has the broom hands it to still another and joins hands with his partner. This continues until the last word of the verse has been sung. Whoever is holding the broom at that moment must keep it.

Chorus: Tra, la, la, la, la

8   All skip around the circle. The child who holds the broom must skip alone in the center of the circle with the broom as his partner.

Repeat several times.

Come, Let Us Be Joyful (German)

Childhood Rhythms Records
Series VIII, Record 805-806

Fine

FORMATION

Sets of four dancers (two couples) arranged in a circle around the room. In each set, partners are side by side and couples face each other.

MEASURES

2   All walk forward three steps (right, left, right) and curtsy.

2   All walk three steps backward to places (left, right, left) and curtsy.

2   Repeat first two measures.

2   Repeat second two measures.

4   Partners link right arms and swing with eight skipping steps.

4   Repeat, linking left arms.

2   All walk forward three steps (right, left, right) and curtsy.

2   All walk three steps backward to places (left, right, left).

4   All walk forward eight steps, passing the opposite couple (going to the right of the dancer directly opposite) and form a new set with the next couple met.

Repeat entire dance with new couple.

CHILDHOOD RHYTHMS

The Donkey Dance (Mexican)

Childhood Rhythms Records
Series X, Record 1003-1004

FORMATION

Children stand side by side in a line or in a single circle, with hands joined.

MEASURES

4 Cross left foot in front of right, then step to the side with the right foot. Do this four times (cross and step, cross and step, cross and step, cross and step), the last time touching the right foot to the side instead of stepping on it.

4 Repeat, crossing right foot in front of left.

8 Jump three times in place, once with right heel forward, once with left heel forward, and once with right heel forward. Do this four times starting alternately with right and left heel forward.

CHILDHOOD RHYTHMS

Feet to Music (American)

Childhood Rhythms Records
Series X, Record 1001-1002

FORMATION

Partners side by side, boys on the left of girls.

Sing as you dance

MEASURES

2   "Feet to music, tap, tap, tap, tap"
On the words "tap, tap, tap, tap," stamp four times left, right, left, right.

2   "Hands with pleasure, clap, clap, clap, clap"
On the words "clap, clap, clap, clap," clap hands four times.

2   "Eyes to see, now look and see"
Place right hand above eyes. On the word "see," bend and look forward. On the word "look," bend and look to the right. On the word "see," bend and look to the left.

2   "Who's the one to dance with me?"
Face partner and slowly make a bow.

1   "Tra, la, la" through the whole music of the song.
Face partner, join both hands. Girl starts with the right foot, boy with the left. Step to the side, bring both feet together, then bend knees and straighten. This is called "step and bend."

7   Continue, alternating left and right six times, then slowly make a bow.

The Grandma Dance (American)

Childhood Rhythms Records
Series X, Record 1001-1002

ALLEGRO MODERATO (♩=96)

FORMATION

Partners side by side, inside hands joined and held together at shoulder height.

Sing as you dance

MEASURES

2 "I will show you how to dance
As my grandma used to do"
Starting with the outside foot (foot farther from partner), walk forward three times, then point the inside toe.

2 Repeat, starting with the inside foot.

2 "I will make a bow to you
As my grandma used to do"
Starting with the outside foot, walk three steps forward, then face partner and bow.

2 Repeat, starting with the inside foot.

CHILDHOOD RHYTHMS

German Clap Dance

Childhood Rhythms Records
Series X, Record 1003-1004

FORMATION

Double circle, partners side by side, inside hands joined, all facing counterclockwise.

MEASURES

3	Starting with the outside foot run twelve steps around the circle in time to the music.
1	Face partners and stamp three times, right, left, right.
1	Point right toe and shake right finger at partner three times.
1	Point left toe and shake left finger.
2	Join right hands and run around partner to place.

CHILDHOOD RHYTHMS

Kanafaska (Moravian)

Childhood Rhythms Records
Series X, Record 1005-1006

FORMATION

Four couples in a square set, all facing center.

```
        G  B
          1
    B 4      2 G
    G    3     B
        B  G
```

MEASURES

2   In a social dancing position, couples 1 and 3 change places with four slides (boys pass back to back).

2   Couples 2 and 4 do the same thing.

2   Couples 1 and 3 return to place with four slides.

2   Couples 2 and 4 return to place with four slides.

8   All dance eight polka steps around the square. On the last count, the boys lift their partners high (the girls jump to make this even higher).

1   Everyone faces center and the first boy walks two steps to the second girl.

7   The first boy and second girl dance six polka steps around the inside of the square, then the boy lifts the girl high as she returns to her place.

16   The first boy repeats this with the third, then with the fourth girl.

72   The second, third, and fourth boys repeat last three steps with each girl in turn (24 measures for each boy).

Knytnarspolska (Danish)

Childhood Rhythms Records
Series X, Record 1005-1006

ALLEGRO (♩=104)

FORMATION

Double circle, partners facing, both hands joined.

MEASURES

4   Moving to the right around a little circle with partner, and starting with right foot, take two slides (count—slide and slide). Cross the left foot in front of the right and hop on it (count—and cross). Do this three times, then stamp three times in place (right, left, right).

Slide and slide and cross
Slide and slide and cross
Slide and slide and cross
Stamp, stamp, stamp

4   Repeat all, moving to the left and starting with left foot.

1 Hands on hips, jump, landing on both feet, turning back to partner.

1 Jump again, turning to face partner.

1 Jump again, turning back to partner and clap three times.

1 Jump again, turning to face partner and clap three times.

2 Partners join both hands, and pulling slightly away swing around to the right and back in place.

2 Repeat to left.

Kolo (Yugoslavian)

Childhood Rhythms Records
Series X, Record 1003-1004

FORMATION

Dancers stand side by side in lines of ten or twelve, with hands on each others' shoulders.

MEASURES

2   Step to the side with the right foot. Step across behind the right foot with the left foot. Step again to the side with the right foot. Raise the left leg forward and across the right, hopping at the same time.

2   Repeat, starting with a step to the side with the left foot.

4   Repeat all, first right, then left.

1   Step to the side with the right foot. Raise the left leg forward and across the right, hopping at the same time.

1   Repeat, starting with a step to the side with the left foot.

2   Repeat all, first right, then left.

4   Step to the side with the right foot. Step across behind the right foot with the left foot. Do this all three times, then step to the side with the right foot, and raise the left leg forward and across the right, hopping at the same time.

4   Repeat, starting with a step to the side with the left foot.

Mexican Social Dance

Childhood Rhythms Records
Series VI, Record 601-602

FORMATION

Couples, partners facing, hands on partners' shoulders.

MEASURES

1 Jump in place three times, touching alternate feet forward (right, left, right).

1 Repeat, starting with left foot (left, right, left).

6 Repeat first two measures, alternating right and left.

4 Link right elbows and skip around partners (eight steps).

4 Link left elbows and repeat.

Nigarespolska (*Danish*)

Childhood Rhythms Records
Series X, Record 1001-1002

FORMATION

Single circle, all facing the center. One child stands in the center of the circle.

MEASURES

4   Place hands on hips. Hop, placing right heel obliquely forward. Hop again, placing left heel forward. Hop again with the right and again with the left heel forward.

8   All clap hands once. The child in the center of the circle runs around the inside of the circle keeping time to the music (three steps to a measure). At the end of the eighth measure this child stops in front of another child and stamps first the right foot, then the left.

4   Repeat the first four measures, with the child in the center facing the child before whom he stopped.

8   Repeat next eight measures. All clap hands once. The child who came from the center of the circle turns his back to the child he was facing. This second child places his hands on the shoulders of the one who faced him. These two children then run around the inside of the circle. At the end of the eighth measure these two children stop in front of another child and stamp first the right foot then the left.

Each time the dance is repeated another child is added to the group moving in the center of the circle.

Old Welsh Dance

Childhood Rhythms Records
Series X, Record 1005-1006

FORMATION

Single circle, partners facing.

MEASURES

1   All step sideward with the right foot (count 1), cross the left foot behind the right and at the same time raise the right foot forward (count 2), then hop on the left foot (count 3).

2   Repeat twice.

1   Step sideward with the right foot (count 1), point the left toe forward (count 2), and hold (count 3).

4   Repeat all, starting with the left foot.

8   Repeat all with the right, then with the left foot.

1   In a double circle with partners side by side, boys facing clockwise and girls counterclockwise, starting with right foot, all run three steps forward.

1   Point the left toe forward (count 1), lift the left foot across in front of the right foot (count 2), swing the left foot forward and hop on it (count 3).

14   Repeat last two measures seven times, alternating left and right.

Patty Cake Polka (American)

Childhood Rhythms Records
Series VIII, Record 801-802

ALLEGRO MODERATO ($\quad$=100)

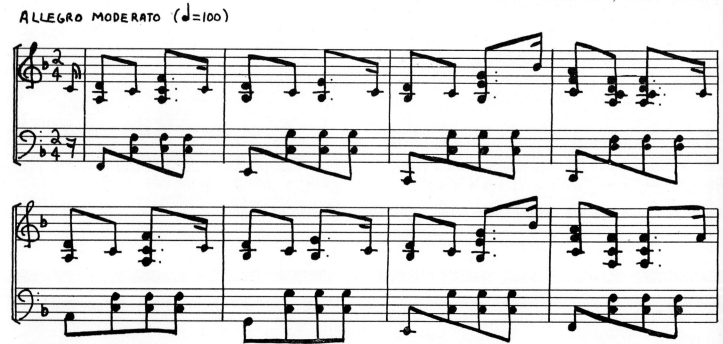

FORMATION

Double circle, partners facing, social dancing position.

MEASURES

1   Boy starts with left foot, girl with right. Touch heel to side (toe up) then touch toe directly in front of other foot. Hop on each of these counts.

1   Repeat first measure.

2   Take four slides to the right (boys' left).

4   Repeat all with other foot.

1   Clap partner's right hand three times.

1   Clap partner's left hand three times.

1   Clap partner's two hands three times.

1   Slap own knees three times.

2   Partners link right elbows and walk four steps around one another.

2   Link left elbows and repeat.

Seven Steps (German Counting Game)

Childhood Rhythms Records
Series VIII, Record 805-806

FORMATION

Double circle, partners side by side, all facing counterclockwise.

MEASURES

2   Start with the right foot and take seven light running steps forward (seventh step is a jump).

2   Repeat, moving backward.

1   Partners turn back to back and take three running steps in the direction they now face (third step is a jump).

1   Turn to face partners, and repeat last measure, moving toward partner.

2   Swing partner for eight counts.

1 Partners turn back to back and take three running steps in the direction they now face (third step is a jump).

1 Turn to face partners and repeat last measure, moving toward partner.

2 Girls move forward one position, boys move back one position, then all swing new partners for eight counts.

Repeat entire dance with new partner.

Six-hand Reel (Irish)

Childhood Rhythms Records
Series X, Record 1005-1006

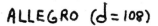

FINE

D.C. AL FINE

FORMATION

Sets of six, partners facing

G G G
B B B

MEASURES

4 Starting with the right foot all do two two-steps forward and two back to place.

4 Repeat all.

4 The three dancers in each line join hands in a small circle, and all do four two-steps around the circle to the right.

4 Repeat last four measures to the left.

4   Dancers return to positions in lines, and the middle dancer in each line links left arms with the one on the left and does four two-steps around to place.

4   The middle dancer links right arms with the one on the right and does four two-steps around to place.

4   All join right hands across forming a big star. All do four two-steps around the star (starting with the right foot).

4   Dancers in each line join hands again in a small circle and do four two-steps around to place.

8   Repeat all, joining left hands to form the big star.

4   Partners join both hands and do four two-steps around each other to the right.

4   Repeat, to the left.